30 DAYS TO BOLD

Joie Miller

 Published in Canonsburg, PA by Champion Center Publishing. ISBN 978-1-7360420-1-4

Welcome to 30 days of Bold!

The wicked flee though no one pursues, but the righteous are as bold as a lion!
Proverbs 28:1 (NIV)

The word **bold** means to be confident and courageous. Boldness is actually the opposite of fearfulness. As a child of God, to be bold is more than just a personality trait. Boldness is something that comes from spending time with God each day, reading His word, and walking in step with the Holy Spirit. I believe that now, more than ever before, we need the boldness that comes from heaven!

God is calling us to boldly stand for righteousness, to boldly live lives that are marked by the God we serve, and to pray bold prayers to see God's will in heaven be done on earth! As you begin this devotional, I pray that your faith is built through the Word, that you grow more confident from spending time with Him, and that you become bold enough to let go of some things and grow!

xoxo- Joie

Day 1 - Self Check

"Search me, God and know my heart; test me and know my anxious thoughts. See if there is any offensive way in me and lead me in the way everlasting." Psalm 139:23-24 (NIV)

There is a safeguard in self-examination. Have you ever wondered how you got so far off track spiritually? Your spiritual walk doesn't die overnight. There are safeguards you can take and symptoms you can be aware of to keep from becoming a stale and stagnant Christian.

The Apostle Paul writes in 1 Corinthians 10:12 (NIV), "So, if you think you are standing firm, be careful that you don't fall." It is important to continually check the condition of your heart. Paul admonished us to stay diligent and self-disciplined.

In 1 Corinthians 9:27(ESV), he says, "I (Paul) remain disciplined in every way so that after preaching to others, I myself am not disqualified from the prize." If the apostle Paul had to continually keep

himself on track, chances are we better check ourselves too! We have to continually be positioning ourselves and checking the condition of our heart to stay in a relationship with our Lord, not allowing ourselves to become deceived by religious form!

Ask yourself:

1. Am I spending time in God's presence and in the Word?
2. Am I serving in God's house?

3. Are the motives and desires of my heart pure?

Don't be afraid to take inventory of your spiritual life. Make any needed adjustments, and then, continue to press onward in your faith!

Declare:

I am spritually strong and attentive to the voice of the Holy Spirit

Day 2 - To Do Hard Things

"Though the righteous fall seven times, they rise again." Proverbs 24:16 (NIV)

You are fashioned for victory, not defeat!

Because of Jesus you are set up to win in every situation! There is nothing that can come at you that Jesus hasn't already provided the way for you to overcome. So, be bold enough to set your mind in winning mode. Whatever situation you are up against today, remember:

> *You are smarter than you think. You have the mind of Christ and the wisom that comes from the Holy Spirit. 1 Corinthians 2:16*
>
> *You are stronger than you feel. You can do all things through Christ who is your strength. When you feel like giving up, tap into your source of strength. When you feel like giving up, tap into your source of sustenance. Phillippians 4:13.*
>
> *You are more anointed than you realize. The same anointing and power that Jesus walked in is accessible to you to overcome and do great works for the kingdom! 1 John 2:27*

Remember, you may come up against hard things, but don't you dare accept defeat! The only way you can lose is by giving up, so keep going because you are fashioned for victory.

Keep getting up!

Declare:

I am anointed to do hard things.

Day 3 - Break the Cycle

"Do not be conformed to this world, but be transformed by the renewal of your mind, that by testing you may discern what is the will of God, what is good and acceptable and perfect." Romans 12:2 (ESV)

"I appeal to you therefore, brothers, by the mercies of God, to present your bodies as a living sacrifice, holy and acceptable to God, which is your spiritual worship." Hebrews 12:1 (ESV)

Have you ever stepped back from your life and noticed there is a pattern that you fall into? You progress forward in your walk with God, and then, all of a sudden you experience the same setbacks like clockwork? The negative cycles in your life need to end this year!

If you are going to move forward in the things of God and break new barriers in your life, you need to recognize what it is that draws you back into old patterns of thinking and living. Ask the Lord to show you what feeds your cycle--sin, discouragement, fear, relationships, etc. Then,

purposefully guard your heart and mind against it. You are in control of your life, not the things that try to beset you or trip you up.

The devil is crafty but not creative; he sees what bait lures you back into old patterns and uses the same strategy every time. When you get a thought or a temptation that Satan knows will draw you back into an old pattern, resist it! Replace that thought or lie with scripture, and then thank God for giving you the breakthrough.

You are breaking negative cycles in your life starting today in Jesus' Name!

Declare:

I am a new creation
in Christ Jesus;
the old is gone, and
all things are new!

Day 4 - Move On (From the Past)

"I thank Christ who has given me strength to do His work. He considered me trustworthy and appointed me to serve him, even though I used to blaspheme the name of Christ. But God had mercy on me and used me as a prime example of his great patience with even the worst sinners. They will realize they can believe in him too and receive eternal life." 1 Timothy 1:12-15 (NLT)

Paul not only was vocal about not believing in the Lord before his salvation, but he even persecuted Christians!

Paul was considered trustworthy once he came to know the Lord, despite his past. In fact, according to Paul, it was his past that became the loudest testimony of God's forgiveness and ability to redeem and use the worst of sinners.

Don't get caught up in who you used to be. Like Paul, let your past be the loudest testimony of God's ability to change a life!

God hasn't disqualified you for doing great things for him, so don't disqualify yourself.

Know you have been redeemed and live a life worthy of the one who redeemed you!

Declare:

I forget what is behind
and focus on what
is ahead in Christ.

Day 5 - Forgiveness

"Be kind and compassionate to one another, forgiving each other, just as in Christ God forgave you." Ephesians 4:32 (NIV)

Be bold enough to forgive. Don't let unforgiveness have residence one more day in your life! If you let it, unforgiveness will be your greatest spiritual and physical hindrance this year.

Nothing will choke out progress like choosing to hold onto an offense. Remember it is a choice! You will choose to let the person who hurt you to be your master, or you will choose to let go and forgive. The hurt is most likely real and legitimate, but the minute you choose to forgive, God can begin to heal your heart. You can't compartmentalize bitterness and unforgiveness, it will begin to define who you are, seeping into your actions, attitudes, and words. It will even affect your health!

Jesus knew we would have to deal with hurt and offense. After all, He did too. In Matthew 5:44, He gives us foolproof instruction on how to keep offense and bitterness from dominating our lives- love your enemies and pray for those who do wrong to you.

This keeps your heart pure and ready to receive all that God has in store. Start today by asking the Lord if there are any areas of unforgiveness you need to let go of today.

Be bold enough to be free!

Declare:

I refuse to be held back
by offense today--
I am love

Day 6 - Keep Sowing

"And let us not grow weary of doing good, for in due season we will reap, if we do not give up." Galatians 6:9 (ESV)

The response when we don't see immediate breakthrough in our lives is to back off the good seed we are sowing.

This is the absolute worst thing you can do! Galatians 6:9 tells us that we will grow weary when we are doing good. When we choose to forgive, tithe, take our thoughts captive, serve others, etc., it is easy to try to justify quitting when you don't see immediate results.

Do not back off! The enemy wants you to become discouraged and quit because he knows if you keep doing what God's word says, you are guaranteed a harvest. If discouragement tries to come, it's a sure sign that you're really close to your breakthrough.

Decide that you will not quit doing good!
And then, keep sowing! Continue to do good! When you start to see success--don't back off but keep sowing seed for your next harvest. It's easy to adapt to a mindset of "I got my breakthrough and now I'm going to back off a little bit" but remember your today determines your tomorrow. Whatever got you the fruit you desire, keep it up!

KEEP SOWING--you will reap a harvest!

Declare:

I will continue to do the good
I know to do even
when I don't feel like it

Day 7 - Inquire of the Lord

"I sought the Lord, and He answered me and delivered me from all my fears." Psalm 34:4 (ESV)

All throughout the Old Testament, Israel's success and defeat was always determined by if they would inquire of the Lord. In 1 Samuel 30, David didn't know what to do because the enemy had stolen their possessions and had taken the women and children. His men wanted to kill him--talk about a bad day. The Bible says that David didn't know what to do so he inquired of the Lord.

We are really good at complaining to God when things don't work out, but do we inquire or get direction from Him daily?

The key to your best life is knowing you are right in the center of God's purpose and plan! Allow God to speak to you about what His assignment is for your life. The most fruitful life is found when you know what the Lord has

for you to do, and you walk in it! In John 15:8 (NIV), Jesus said, "It's to my Father's glory that you produce much fruit, then they will know you are my disciples." If you struggle finding purpose, or if you're frustrated because you want to bear more fruit for the kingdom--inquire of the Lord!

The Holy Spirit will reveal God's will to you. You will be led by peace, instruction from the word, or maybe even a confirmation from a friend or pastor. God doesn't hide his plan from you, so ask!

Declare:

I position my heart
to hear and obey
God's voice today

Day 8 - Choose Righteousness

"The eyes of the Lord are on the righteous, and he is attentive to their cry." Psalm 34:15 (NIV)

Living a life of righteousness is a choice that we have because of Jesus. The Bible says that before Jesus, even on your best day you would fall short. But through Jesus, we are now empowered to say no to sin.

Romans 6:16 says, "Sin is no longer your master, for you no longer live under the requirements of law. Instead, you live under the freedom of God's grace." Sin will always fight to be your master, it's the grace of God that came to EMPOWER you to walk in freedom. The grace of God enables you to overcome the power of sin and walk in the truth of God's Word.

Grace doesn't give us an excuse to sin, after all our flesh will find enough excuses on its own, but a bigger *Yes* to respond to, and that is a relationship with Jesus.

Grace allows me to choose Jesus over temptation. Through His power, we can overcome any struggle that comes our way. The next time temptation comes knocking at your door, remember you have a choice: choose Jesus!

Declare:

I am the righteousness of God through Christ Jesus

Day 9 - Hope

"We have this hope as an anchor for the soul, firm and secure." Hebrews 6:19 (NIV)

Our soul is where our mind, will, and emotions live. Often, when we are believing God for something in faith, our soul needs to be reminded of the Hope of who Jesus is. When it's tempting to try to figure things out, renew your mind with the word of God. The word will build your faith in who Jesus is and what He is able to do.

Hope produces faith!

Hope isn't a wish; Biblical hope is in Jesus Christ and the promise we have in Him. When we anchor our prayer life in the Word, we are creating a substantiated faith that springs up from the hope that we have in His promises. (Colossians 1:5)

Anchoring your prayer in scripture creates a tangible faith that can't go unnoticed by heaven.

Get in the Word and pray from scripture, and you can have full assurance your prayers will be answered!

Declare:

I am led by the Spirit and not by my emotions

Day 10 - Rest

"I was glad when they said to me, let us go to the house of the Lord." Psalms 122:1 (NLT)

One thing that should be on your agenda every Sunday is going to the house of God!

In Exodus 20, the Lord tells us to observe the Sabbath day and make it holy. In the busy age that we live in, it becomes easy to try to justify Sunday as a day of relaxation. Life has us so busy that we can begin to rationalize sleeping in on Sunday or spending the day as a family, rather than attending church.

A few hours out of your week to honor the Lord will change the whole direction of your life and family. It's amazing how going to church and hearing God's word, and then applying that word can eliminate most of the things that cause you stress and hardship throughout the week!

God didn't set up the Sabbath to take away your day of rest but rather, going to church and being refreshed in the Word actually rejuvenates you--even more than sleeping in! The Sabbath was created for man, not man for the Sabbath, so enjoy the blessing of what God intended to keep you refreshed!

Declare:

I am faithful to
be in the House of God
and count it a joy

Day 11 - Sound Mind

"For God has not given us a spirit of fear, but of power and of love and of a sound mind."
2 Timothy 1:7 (NKJV)

In most Bible translations, sound mind is translated into the word self-discipline. A sound mind starts with being disciplined about what thoughts we think about. Every thought that you think isn't worthy of meditation. In fact, some thoughts just need to be immediately rejected. How do you know the difference? Through renewing your mind with God's Word.

The Bible tells us that when we renew our mind with what God says, then we will know His good, pleasing, and perfect will for our lives. Once I know what God thinks about a matter, I can clearly measure if my thoughts are lining up with Him or if they are thoughts that come from my own opinions- or even lies from the enemy.

Taking your thoughts captive to the obedience of Christ starts with a decision. Today, decide that you aren't going to think about things that are contrary to what God says about you. Replace lies with truth, and remember you have the ability to steer clear of destructive thoughts!

Take your thoughts captive, or they will take you captive!

Declare:

I take every thought captive to the obedience of Christ

Day 12 - Take God at His Word

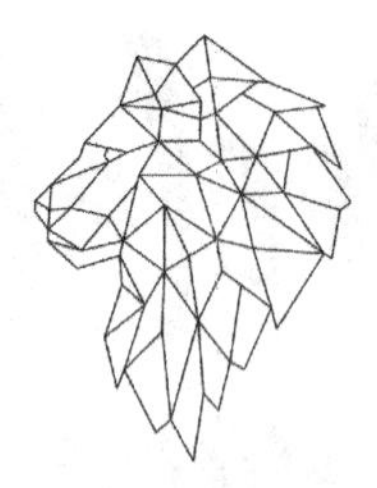

"God is not man, that He should lie, or a son of man, that He should change his mind. Has He said, and will He not do it? Or has He spoken, and will He not fulfill it?" Numbers 23:19 (ESV)

Jeremiah 33:20-22 reminds us that as sure as the sun will rise and set, we can be that sure that God will keep His covenant to us. When is the last time you lay in bed worrying if the sun would rise in the morning? Do you fret all day wondering if evening will actually come? No, of course not.

The sun rising and setting are laws of nature. We are so convinced that the law will do what it's intended to do that we don't even give thought to it. This is how confident we should be that what God promised will come to pass.

"Then the Lord said to me, "You have seen well, for I am (actively) watching over My word to fulfill it." Jeremiah 1:12 (AMP)

Stop wasting time and energy worrying and fretting about a situation, and instead, declare God's word over it! He is not a man that He should lie, if He spoke it- He will bring it to pass!

Declare:

Every promise God spoke over my life will come to pass

Day 13 - Faith

On the third day a wedding took place at Cana in Galilee. Jesus' mother was there, and Jesus and his disciples had also been invited to the wedding. When the wine was gone, Jesus' mother said to him, "They have no more wine.""Woman, why do you involve me?" Jesus replied. "My hour has not yet come."His mother said to the servants, "Do whatever he tells you."

Nearby stood six stone water jars, the kind used by the Jews for ceremonial washing, each holding from twenty to thirty gallons. Jesus said to the servants, "Fill the jars with water"; so, they filled them to the brim. Then he told them, "Now draw some out and take it to the master of the banquet."They did so, and the master of the banquet tasted the water that had been turned into wine. He did not realize where it had come from, though the servants who had drawn the water knew. Then he called the bridegroom aside and said, "Everyone brings out the choice wine first and then the cheaper wine after the guests have had too much to drink; but you have saved the best till now." What Jesus did here in Cana of Galilee was the first of the signs through which he revealed his glory; and his disciples believed in him. John 2:1-11 (NIV)

Though Jesus said it wasn't time yet to manifest a miracle, Mary's faith was like a magnet for the miraculous. Faith produces a supernatural demand on God's power that heaven can't ignore! It was Mary's faith in who she knew Jesus to be, and what she knew He could do, that brought forth His first miracle recorded in the Bible. Her faith in Jesus put a demand on heaven.

Not too long ago I saw my daughter Mia hanging out by the front door. I asked her what she was doing, and she responded, "I'm waiting for my package to arrive." She hadn't physically ordered anything, but by faith she was believing for a certain toy to be delivered. Her confidence in God's ability to answer her prayer caused me to order it for her. Her faith in God put a draw on me to respond. Her faith was like a magnet to her miracle.

Believe God in a way that your faith in who He is, and what you know He can do, demands a miraculous response from Heaven!

Declare:

today is the day for my miracle

Day 14 - Joy

"You will go out in joy and be led forth in peace." Isaiah 55:12 (NIV)

Joy is your portion as a child of God! Joy is one of the marks of the kingdom of God on your life. (Romans 14:17) Happiness is a feeling, it comes from your soul. Joy is a fruit; it comes out of your spirit (Galatians 5:22) This is why you can be going through something very difficult and still have joy. Joy is not circumstantial; it can be a constant in your life--if you choose for it to be. If you struggle walking in joy, ask yourself:

1. Am I being refreshed in God's presence?

Doing life without spending time in prayer leads to weariness and discouragement. A fruit of the spirit is produced by spending time with God.

2. Am I renewing my mind in the Word of God?

If you're not renewing your mind, it will align with thoughts that are contrary to scripture and can leave us feeling hopeless and discouraged.

3. Am I giving thanks to the Lord?

Keeping your heart thankful for what the Lord has done will increase your expectancy for the good things ahead.

Let the joy of the Lord be your strength today!

Declare:

the joy of the Lord is my strength

Day 15 - Enjoy Today

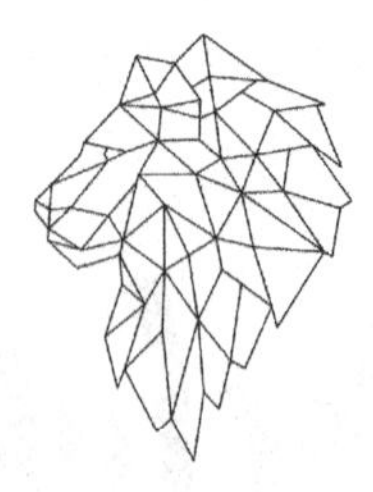

"This is the day the Lord has made; let us rejoice and be glad in it." Psalm 118:24 (ESV)

Stay in stride with what the Lord is doing in your life today! The enemy loves to distract you by having you focus on either the past or the future. Maybe it's a thought of regret or hurt from a past season, or maybe it's the lie that your best days were behind you. If not thinking of the past, maybe it's continually worrying about the future- or the discontentment of "I just can't wait until mindset."

You just can't wait until you're married or until you have kids, there's always something next that's more exciting. Maybe it's not even excitement about the future, but rather the distraction of worrying about what's going to happen next. The Bible says not to worry about tomorrow, don't get ahead of where God has you.

He'll lead you to where you need to be! No worrying allowed! In Matthew 6:34, God actually commands us not to worry. If he gives us a command, it means He has also graced us with the power to say no to the worry. Then, in
Isaiah 43:18, he tells us to stop meditating on the past--you're not there anymore. You can't change it, so learn from it and move on.

That leaves us to enjoy today. Enjoy what God is doing in the now, acknowledge it, and thank Him for it! Rest in the fact that He has a good plan for you and good works set apart for you to accomplish. You have a faithful Father who will guide you along the way. Don't miss God's plan unfolding in your life TODAY!

Declare:

I will rejoice in today because it is a gift from God

Day 16 - Obedience

"Obedience is better than sacrifice." I Samuel 15:22 (NLT)

Always go with God's plan! When the Lord speaks instruction and direction to you, be quick to obey. Obedience to what He is telling you to do yields blessing and clarity for your life.

When Elisha received God's direction in 1 Kings 19:19, he went out and broke his plow and then burned it. There was no resorting back to Plan B for Elisha! Elisha was making a statement to God that he was all in. Jonah on the other hand ran from God's plan in disobedience. Jonah took himself out of a place of peace and protection.

As scary as it may seem, God's way is always best. Don't wait until you're comfortable or at a place where everything makes complete sense in your mind to obey. When you hear his voice, obey quickly.

An outward expression of your faith is your willingness to take steps of obedience. Are there areas in your life you have tried to ignore God's promptings like Jonah? Do you feel stuck or somehow out of step with God's plan?

Ask God for wisdom and direction and He will answer. Sometimes it's as simple as going back to the last thing He told you to do and simply doing it. Don't delay- just obey!

Declare:

When I hear your voice, I am quick to obey

Day 17 - Choose to Serve

"But as for me and my house, we will serve the LORD." Joshua 24:15 (ESV)

God always allows us to decide. The people of Israel were given a choice. They could go on serving the idols of their ancestors or they could destroy their false gods and serve the Lord.

Joshua made a declaration that no matter what everyone else decided, his family would serve the Lord.

This is great news because this means that you aren't bound to your past or to your family history--you get to choose! I've known people who have been raised in Christian homes all their lives and have chosen to walk away from the Lord.

Also, like myself, I know people who didn't have a godly heritage that chose to live for God and to raise their family in the faith.

No matter what your past is, no matter what your family is like, no matter how many mistakes you've made, no matter what everyone else in the world is doing, you can make the same decision and declaration as Joshua--that as for me and my house, we will serve the Lord.

Declare:

As for me and my house, we will serve the Lord

Day 18 - Connection

"As iron sharpens iron, so one person sharpens another." Proverbs 27:17 (NIV)

It matters who you connect yourself with. In 1 Timothy 6:11-16, Paul is provoking Timothy to fight the fight of faith. He gives him encouragement and instruction to be everything God has called Timothy to be. Paul was compelling, even propelling, Timothy forward. Who you choose to connect with in life will affect the way you run your race too.

I have heard it said that the people around you will either act as propellers or anchors in your life. Just as connecting with the wrong people can hinder, or keep you stuck, connecting with the right people will propel you. There should be relationships in your life that will propel you further into what God has for you. Paul made it part of his mission to see that Timothy would succeed in the Lord.

May the Lord bring people into your life this year that will make it their mission to see you succeed. Joining yourself to people who believe in what God has called you to do, and have gone before you with success, will bring you spiritual strength and momentum to grow to full potential this year.

Identify these people, invest in these relationships, and watch how the Lord uses them to bring strength and increase into your life!

Declare:
My relationships propel my forward in my faith

Day 19 - Resolve

"When he arrived and saw what the grace of God had done, he was glad and encouraged them all to remain true to the Lord with all their hearts." Acts 11:23 (NIV)

Live resolved! If you're going to do anything to increase your boldness this year, you must live resolved. Being resolved starts with a decision. Paul writes in Hebrews to fix our eyes on Jesus, the author and perfecter of our faith. No matter what happens this year, you need to stay fixed, or resolved in Jesus - firm and steadfast.

There are three areas of our lives that we must watch over to stay resolved. The first area is in your mind. Renew your mind in the word and refuse to dwell on thoughts contrary to it!

The second area is in your speech. Even when you don't feel like your faith is at work, whatever you do, don't speak it or your own words will abort your blessing. Lastly, stay resolved in spirit.
No matter what trial comes, don't give up--learn to fight the fight of faith.

Giving up is not an option!

Declare:

I will not waver in my faith

Day 20 - Hearing God's Voice

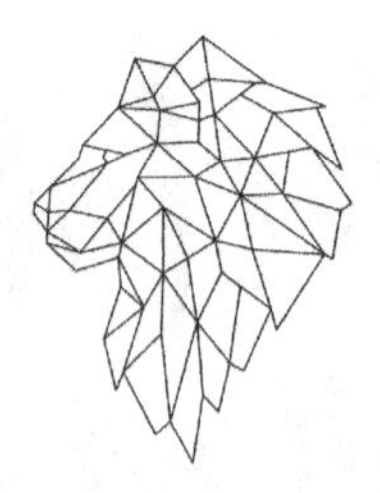

"Speak Lord, your servant is listening." 1 Samuel 3:9 (NLT)

God's sheep know his voice.

How do you know what you're hearing is or isn't from the Lord? Jesus said His sheep would know His voice. Learn to discern between God's voice, and the voices of others, self, or even the enemy. When you train yourself to know God's voice it will eliminate confusion and frustration in your walk with God. There are ways that you can begin to grow in confidence as you hear God's voice.

Here are some tips to help refine your ear:

1.The voice of God never contradicts the Bible. If it's not in God's word or if it's contrary to the principles in scriptures, you're not hearing God's voice. (John 10:27)

2. God's voice never leaves you feeling depressed or hopeless. Even when the Lord is correcting something in your life, He always leaves you feeling hopeful, at peace, and loved by Him. (Romans 2:4)

3. His voice leads us, instructs us, and gives us a way out of situations that cause harm or temptation to us. His voice never condemns, degrades, or gives up on us! (Romans 8:1)

4. God's voice and instruction will produce the marks of the kingdom on your life - righteousness, peace, and joy. (Romans 14:7)

Live your day with your heart and spirit open to hear from Him, He will answer!

Declare:

I hear and recognize God's voice with clarity

Day 21 - Staying Strong

"I have told you these things, so that in me you may have peace. In this world you will have trouble. But take heart! I have overcome the world." John 16:33 (NIV)

This is a great reminder that if you're going through This is a great reminder that if you're going through trouble, it doesn't mean you have weak faith, nor does it mean the trouble should weaken your faith.

The world we live in sometimes brings adversity, but through Jesus we always have victory!

Some people camp out in the first half of that verse thinking life is full of ups and downs, and life on this side of eternity will always be a struggle.

But the second half of the verse promises that there is nothing that Jesus hasn't paid the price and paved the way for you to overcome too.

So, stay strong! Your trial doesn't define you; victory is your portion!

Declare:

I go from strength to strength and from victory to victory

Day 22 - Fear

"Fear not, for I am with you; be not dismayed, for I am your God; I will strengthen you. I will help you, I will uphold you with my righteous right hand." Isaiah 41:10 (ESV)

False Evidence Appearing Real.

Often the spirit of fear is just that, false evidence that is seemingly a reality. It comes in the form of intimidation of what may happen and speaks lies of intimidation. Silence the voice of fear in your life! Faith and fear cannot coexist. Fear actually hinders your prayers.

Prayers birthed out of fear aren't prayed in faith. When you operate out of a spirit of fear, your faith in that which you are afraid of is greater than your faith in God. Fear paralyzes you spiritually.

The people of Israel in 1 Samuel 17 were paralyzed by fear and a daunting Goliath.
The enemy used fear and intimidation to hold God's people back from operating in their true identity and authority. Faith over fear says, I know who my God is, and I know He is greater than anything or anyone that tries to come against me!

Don't let fear take hold of you. Know your God and walk in perfect peace of mind.

Declare:

I don't operate in fear,
but in power, love,
and a sound mind

Day 23 - Control Your Soul

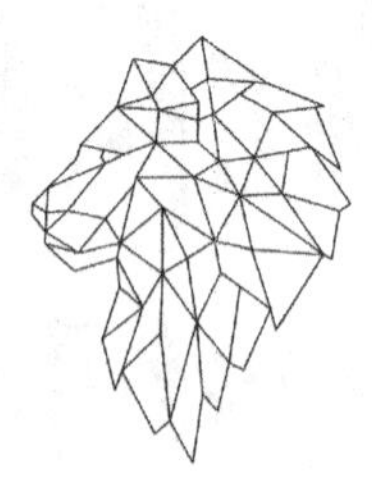

"For God alone, O my soul, wait in silence, for my hope is from Him." Psalm 62:5 (ESV)

You can control your soul! Your soul is your mind, will, and emotions. When you became a Christian, you no longer had to be led by your emotions and your feelings but by your spirit.

Your soul makes a horrible master, but a wonderful servant. Being led by your soul can leave you chaotic, confused, anxious, or depressed. But when you are led by your spirit, you can always reside in a place of peace, joy, and rest.

By renewing your mind with God's word (Romans 12:2), your soul can be a great asset to your spirit. After all, God didn't create you as a robot--He created you with a beautiful mind and soul.

The secret is not allowing your soul to take lead! Weigh your thoughts against God's word to measure the validity. Bring your emotions under the submission of your spirit.

David did this so well in the Bible. At one point, he even begins to talk to his soulish self. He says, "Why are you downcast o, my soul?" Praise the Lord! David took control of His soul, and you can too!

Declare:

I am led by my spirit man, not by my emotions

Day 24 - Pray Big

"Have faith in God, Jesus answered. Truly I tell you, if anyone says to this mountain, 'Go throw yourself into the sea,' and does not doubt in their heart but believes that what they say will happen, it will be done for them. Therefore I tell you, whatever you ask for in prayer, believe that you have received it, and it will be yours." Mark 11:22-24 (NIV)

What are you praying for? Are your prayers big and bold, or do you feel like you are bothering God or asking too big? Mark 11:22-24 tells us that God wants us to ask big!

The Bible is talking about having the God kind of faith. The faith that we have often limits God based on what we think is possible. God kind of faith operates from God's perspective that nothing is impossible for Him!

Often, we allow our natural thinking and ability to figure out how God is going to do it to limit our ask. Maybe your rationalizing and thinking has even caused a little bit of doubt. Build your faith through reading God's word and by recounting all the ways God has answered your prayers in the past!

Remember, the Bible says that with man it is impossible but with God all things are possible!

Take the limits off!

The next time you are praying, try activating the kind of faith that Mark 11 talks about and ask BIG!

Declare:

I will believe God for the impossible

Day 25 - Get Going

"Do not despise these small beginnings, for the Lord rejoices to see the work begin."
Zechariah 4:10 (NLT)

It's a good time to start moving on that thing that is in your heart to do. Just start! If you're waiting to feel 100% ready, 100% sure, 100% adequate, then chances are you'll just keep waiting!

Faith takes action! Often, I think of my faith like the motion activated doors at the grocery store. I could stand back and stare at the door all day waiting for it to open, but the activation happens when I start moving towards it. Think about the Israelites escaping Egypt in Exodus. When they came to the Red Sea, it looked like a dead end in the natural. When Moses took action and put His staff in the water, the path became clear.

Moses could have sat on the water's edge and wondered why God wasn't making a way for them, but the breakthrough was found in Moses activating his faith. Many times, we sit around waiting on God, but in reality, maybe He is waiting on you.

Remember, God rejoices to see the work begin! Make an effort today to take steps towards your dream, even if it's just an investment of 20 minutes a day.

Get started!

Declare:

I am equipped, anointed,
and ready to move forward
in what God has called
me to do

Day 26 - Dream Big

"Now to him who is able to do immeasurably more than all we could ask or imagine, according to his power that is at work within us." Ephesians 3:20 (NIV)

Be bold enough to dream big! If you can dream it, God can do it! What is the desire that He has placed in your heart? What do you think about before you fall asleep at night? What is the thing that you are always daydreaming about?

In Genesis, God had a BIG plan for Abram. For Abram to understand the vastness of God's thinking, He had to take him outside of His tent to the expanse of the open sky. Are you on the same page as God when it comes to dreaming for the immeasurably more or do you limit God within the boundaries of the tent?

God's plan for you is big! If God has put the desire in your heart, He has also provided the power to see it come to pass!

He fulfills the desires that He gives us! Isn't that beautiful? It takes all the stress off me. I just stay in love with Him and obey His instruction and I will see it come to pass.

Stop doubting yourself and start trusting His work in you. He's given you the desire AND the power to walk in all that He has planned for you. So, start dreaming today. As you dream with God and wrap your faith around His plan for you, He will bring it to pass!

Declare:

God's plan for me is big, and I will see it come to pass!

Day 27 - Lead Strong

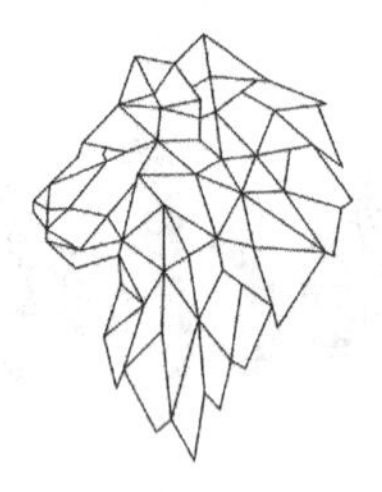

"Being confident of this very thing, that he who began a good work in you will perfect it until the day of Jesus Christ." Philippians 1:6 (ASV)

"Leadership is influence- nothing more, nothing less." John Maxwell

Who are you leading? We all have an area of influence.

Whether you are a teacher, a minister, a business owner, or a parent, you are an influencer; therefore, you are a leader.

Leverage your influence for maximum and lasting impact by growing in leadership.

Read a leadership book, listen to a leadership podcast-- make the investment. As you grow your leadership, your influence will enlarge.

If you get BETTER, your influence will get BIGGER.

Choose to grow!

Declare:

I will leverage my leadership for the glory of God

Day 28 - Expectation

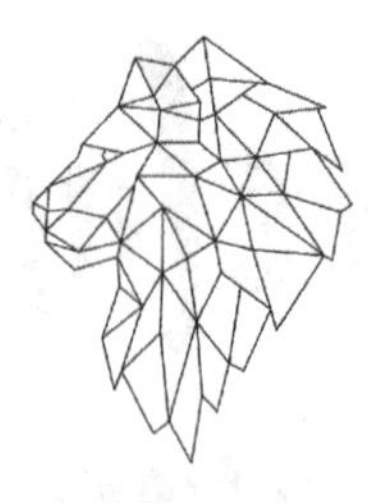

"There is surely a future hope for you, and your hope will not be cut off." Proverbs 23:18 (NIV)

Expectation is an expression of faith. Whatever you expect, you attract.

The Bible warns about foreboding thoughts; these are anxious thoughts of bad things. (Proverbs 15:5) When we meditate on these thoughts, we start to expect that they will happen.

Expectation of bad things yields anxiety.

Instead of meditating on the bad, meditate on the good. Fix your mind on what is good and in God's word and measure your thoughts against truth. Meditating on the good yields peace.

The Bible says that it is peace that guards your heart and mind from anxiety. It also sets your expectation in faith!

Faith over fear, good thoughts over bad, and peace over anxiety! What are you expecting today?

"And now, Lord, what do I wait for and expect? My hope and expectation are in You." Psalm 39:7 (AMP)

Declare:

Goodness and mercy are chasing my down today; I am expecting good things!

Day 29 - Give Thanks

"Call the things that are not as though they are." Romans 4:17 (NKJV)

Thanksgiving is an expression of faith. Think about it, when do you usually thank someone? You thank someone after you have received something from them.

When you go to a restaurant, you express gratitude to the server through a tip after they have served you. What would it say to that server if as soon as you sat down, you pulled out money and tipped them in advance? They would probably think you have a lot of faith in their ability to serve and they wouldn't want to disappoint you.

When you thank God in advance for what you are believing Him for, you are expressing that you have already received it by faith. You are expressing your confidence in who He is and what He will do!

Whatever you focus on, you will attract in your life. An attitude of thankfulness will attract blessing and focus on what is good. Complaining is the opposite of faith. Complaining is like telling God he hasn't done anything for you, and He never will. Thankfulness magnifies the good and builds faith in all that God has done and all He will continue to do!

Give God thanks in advance, and know that as you do, you are activating faith! What can you thank God in advance for today?

Declare:

I will give thanks
to God in
all circumstances

Day 30 - Reach the One

"Go into all the world and preach the gospel to every creature." Mark 16:15 (NKJV)

God loves people; therefore, you should love people. God sees value and potential in every human being. That compels me to ask myself, "What do I see in people?" When we live our lives with an awareness that each and every person's eternity was already paid for by Jesus Christ, it should compel us to share God's love with the lost.

Sharing your faith starts with a burden from God. Ask God today for a burden for those around you who don't know the Lord. Start by praying for the lost who are in your life. This will make you more aware of the opportunities to share your faith when they arise.

Look for ways to use your life as a witness. A simple smile, card, or act of kindness will open the door for the gospel message.

Ask yourself, "What is my circle of influence and how can I be more bold to share my faith?"

Declare:

I have a heart for the lost because they are valuable to God

Heavenly Father,

I thank you for your word that makes us bold! I thank you that as we hide that word in our hearts daily our faith will continue to grow. I pray that we would approach your throne with a new boldness that comes from a relationship with you. I pray that we would pray bold prayers and see them answered in Jesus' Name!

I thank you for the Holy Spirit who lives in us and fills us with power and courage to share our faith with others. I pray that fresh faith would fill us now and that we will be bold enough to stand for what is right and to walk away from every evil thing! Fill us now with your power that we can change the world around us and shine bright for you.

In Jesus' Name, Amen!

Declarations

Use this space to write out your favorite Declarations from 30 Days of Bold.

Made in the USA
Middletown, DE
08 September 2021